MW01257710

Putting God First

How to Make God the #1 Priority in Every Area of Your Life

Brittany Ann

www.equippinggodlywomen.com

Copyright and Disclaimer

Table of Contents

Introduction

Do you ever feel stressed, worn out, exhausted or overwhelmed? Like no matter how hard you work, how late you stay up or how much you plan and multitask, there simply is never enough time to fit it all in? Has quiet time with the Lord become a distant memory? And while you know you should change that, at the end of another long day, all you really want to do is fall into bed and sleep?

Or perhaps you know you have enough time in your day, but you struggle to use it wisely. Whether it's watching television, shopping, connecting on social media or spending time on your latest hobby, your days always seem to escape into thin air. And before you know it, it's been weeks and you haven't opened your Bible at all.

You want to spend time with the Lord. You know it's important. And yet, you constantly find yourself distracted.

As a busy work-at-home mom of two little ones (with one on the way!), I know exactly what it feels like to reach the end of another exhausting day only to realize that I haven't spent any time with God and that, frankly, I'm simply too tired to care. And I run a website for Christian women! I should know better!

But fortunately, I also know just how wonderful and fulfilling life can be when you finally make God your number one priority and shift your life so it fully centers around Him. And that's what I want for you as well.

What would you give to live a life that is characterized by abundant joy, peace, passion and balance? A life that leaves you fulfilled in a way you never thought possible? A life that is full of all the blessings God wants to offer you?

This life can be yours—if you're ready and willing to make God your number one priority.

You see, Christianity isn't supposed to be just a set of rules and regulations. It's not a list of boxes to check off to see if you did a good enough job to make God happy today. *Church on Sunday. Check. Drop an envelope in the offering plate. Check. Enroll your kids in private school, or better yet, homeschool. Check.*

No, Christianity is an exciting adventure, a romantic relationship, an incredible story that winds and weaves throughout the generations. It's a fascinating whirlwind of incredible moments you never dreamed possible. The truth is, God has an amazing journey just waiting for you. And it all starts when you commit to be all in.

Sure, you could continue the way you've been going—focusing your attention on whatever happens to be right in front of you at the moment. It's easy. Convenient. But don't you want so much more?

Don't spend another day simply surviving. Don't settle for good enough. Take hold of the amazing life God has in store for you. This book will show you how.

My prayer for you throughout this book is twofold: one, that you will be inspired to want to make God the center of your life and to embrace all that He has for you, and two, that you will be equipped with the knowledge, tools and resources you need to do just that.

So, are you ready? It's going to be quite the ride.

<u>Section One</u>

The Importance of Putting God First

Chapter 1

The Effects of a Life Out of Control

"We'll need to run a couple of tests," my doctor said, without much emotion. "We'll check you for anemia, and we'll also check your thyroid. Both conditions are common during pregnancy."

Yes, fatigue may be extremely common during pregnancy, but as someone who has always been fortunate enough to have extremely easy pregnancies, I knew something was off. I had spent nearly my entire first trimester lying on the couch all day, letting the house go to shambles and the kids do whatever they pleased. Now, in my second trimester, when I was supposed to be feeling better, I wasn't. At least, not by much.

I was tired all the time, and I wore out way too quickly. Something as small as walking across the playground left me needing to sit down and rest. Tackling my usual weekly trip to the grocery store left me utterly exhausted for the rest of the day. My husband, who has always been helpful, suddenly became incredibly helpful, offering to go to the grocery store, do the laundry, take the kids—whatever I needed so I could get some rest. And now, my doctor wanted blood tests.

I wasn't particularly worried as I headed home that day. Neither condition is that serious and I imagined both would be fairly easy to treat. Frankly, I was just ready to get to the bottom of all of this. What was causing me to be so exhausted all the time?

As I Googled both conditions that weekend, however, neither one really seemed to fit. I didn't have half of the symptoms they listed, and the half that I did have were all easily explained by the fact that I was pregnant. Something else was wrong. And it didn't take long for me to realize what it was, as much as I didn't want to admit it.

Article after article gave the same standard advice—advice that I already knew, but wasn't exactly following. *Eat a healthy diet. Get plenty of sleep. Drink plenty of water. Exercise regularly. Relax and enjoy your pregnancy.* And here I was completely neglecting my own health, working long hours on little sleep, trying to be the perfect wife, the perfect mother, homeschool, keep a clean home, run two blogs and work from home. No wonder I was tired!

But even worse, over the next few weeks, I realized just how out of balance things had become. I used to read my Bible regularly; I wasn't doing that anymore. I was still attending church regularly, but it had become little more than a duty or obligation. I never looked forward to it, and I wasn't getting anything out of it. My quiet times were non-existent, and my prayer life was becoming increasingly shallow and self-centered.

I was grouchy, irritable and distracted with my children far more than I should have been, and my oldest son's behavior was starting to be affected by it. He was starting to get a serious attitude, and I knew exactly where he got it from: me.

I had known for a while that I wasn't giving my husband the attention he deserved, but I didn't realize how badly I'd neglected him until a particularly serious conversation late one night that left me in tears the rest of the weekend.

When I got together with friends and family, I always felt out of the loop. Everyone else seemed to know what was going on in everyone else's lives. They knew just what questions to ask to catch up on all the latest news. I only knew the highlights I had seen on Facebook.

My life was distracted, unbalanced and chaotic. And it was taking a serious toll on my health and on my relationships. I wasn't living the full and abundant life God had planned for me, and it was time for a change.

Chapter 2

Identifying the Root of the Issue

Now, your story may not look exactly like mine. But chances are, you too have something that's coming in between you and the rich and abundant life God has for you. Maybe it's watching too much television. Maybe it's spending too much time on social media. Maybe it's simply your own laziness, selfishness, stubbornness or pride. Whatever it is, each of us has something that threatens to distract us and rob us from all that God has to offer. And it affects us all more than we know.

For me, it was working too much. Not that working is bad, but I had let my goals, worries and ambitions take center stage, pushing everything else to the side in the process. I was relying on myself to make sure everything would turn out okay instead of relying on God, even though He has proven to me time and time again that if I would only relax and trust, He always, always comes through.

For months, I'd been pushing myself harder and faster while neglecting my physical and spiritual health in return. I'd eat a chocolate bar (or several) to stay awake instead of listening to my body and going to bed at a decent hour. I'd neglect rest, relationships and quiet time in favor of churning out a few more articles, replying to a few more blog comments or making a few more tweaks to my site.

I was a woman on a mission, but not the right mission.

And while that worked in the short term, it was never going to stand up over the long term. The fact is, when we don't make God our number one priority, we suffer the consequences, whether we realize it or not. And while it would have been easy for me to say "Oh, a little tiredness is no big deal. It's a normal pregnancy symptom. I'm sure I'm fine." I knew deep down that the real issue was much more serious than that.

For me, it wasn't simply a matter of sleeping a little more or eating a little better (though those things did help). For me, the real issue was a life that had gotten dreadfully out of balance and out of focus when I stopped focusing on God and let myself get distracted by all of the other things I thought were so important instead. Things that really weren't that important at all.

Common Distractions

So, what things are distracting you from the full and abundant life that God has for you? Whether we want to admit it or not, all of us have something that is getting in our way.

Earlier this summer, I conducted a small survey on my website, Equipping Godly Women, to find out more about the spiritual lives of my readers. Which habits and practices most encouraged them and strengthened their faith? What obstacles were getting in their way? What did they most need to help them grow?

In response to the question, "What is the biggest obstacle or challenge preventing you from being the woman God wants you to be?" the most common responses were: laziness, selfishness, busyness, lack of time management, distractions and an inability to focus.

Yep. Been there. I AM there half the time. And I bet you are too. In fact, just check out the following descriptions. Chances are, you'll see yourself in at least one of them.

11

Laziness

You know you should spend time with God, but you never seem to get around to it. You always tell yourself "I'll read my Bible later..." but then you never do. Instead, you fill your free time with cheap entertainment. A few hours of television after dinner, a little mindless scrolling through Pinterest or Facebook before bed... your days go by quickly, but you never seem to know exactly where they went.

Selfishness

You know you should spend time with God, but you don't really care enough to do anything about it. You'd much rather spend your days doing things that are more interesting, more pressing or more important. Your day is full of activities you love, but when you go to bed at night, sometimes you feel guilty for not caring as much as you know you should.

Busyness

You know you should spend time with God, but you just don't know how you could possibly fit another thing in to your already over-scheduled day. From the minute you wake up in the morning until the minute your head hits the pillow at night, you have things to do, places to go and people to see. Your family is constantly clamoring for your attention, you're working more hours than ever and you just can't seem to say no when yet another volunteer committee opportunity arises, even though you know you should. Your days go by quickly, and by the time you even think about God at the end of the day, you're fast asleep before you can even reach for your Bible.

Lack of Time Management

You know you should spend time with God, but your days always seem to escape you. It's not that you're lazy. Rather, your daily tasks take way longer than they should because you can't quite seem to figure out how to balance everything properly. At the end of the day, you still have a handful of things on your to-do list that you never got around to, and spending time with God is always one of them (if it made it on your list at all).

Distractions

You know you should spend time with God, but every time you mean to, you get distracted. Something as simple as "I'd love to enjoy a cup of coffee while I read my Bible" quickly turns into "I'll just put a few dishes away while the coffee's brewing," "I'd better fill up the dog's bowl before I forget," and "What are we having for dinner tonight? I probably need to set something out to thaw..." By the time you do finally open your Bible, your kids are running into the kitchen asking for breakfast. You set your Bible aside for later but never get around to picking it up again.

An Inability to Focus

You know you should spend time with God, but every time you find a minute to sit down in relative peace and quiet, your mind starts wandering. "I wonder what my husband meant when he made that strange comment last night." "I should really call Ann and see how she's doing." "I hope Parker is able to pull his grades up. They're going to kick him off the basketball team if he doesn't, and he's going to be devastated." Before you know it, quiet time is up and you've spent more time worrying about or thinking through future events than you have spent humbling yourself before God.

Honestly, the list of things that can keep us from God is endless. And if it's not one thing, it's another. So not only do we have to first figure out what is standing in our way, but we also need to identify and begin to implement real, practical strategies to help us keep God in the center of our lives right where He belongs. The second section of this book will help you do just that.

Chapter 3

Why Put God First?

Before we can get into the details about how to put God first, though, I think it's important to take a minute to discuss why we should make God a priority in the first place. After all, you don't just center your life around something or someone for no reason.

Of the countless reasons why we could put God first, six major ones immediately come to mind: because He deserves it, because He commands it, so we are available for God-ordained appointments, so we don't miss out on the fullness that God offers, to keep us near to God and because life goes that much better when we do.

Because He Deserves It

"Do you not know that your bodies are temples of the Holy Spirit, who is in you, whom you have received from God? You are not your own; you were bought at a price. Therefore honor God with your bodies." — 1 Corinthians 6:19-20

As responsible adults free to make our own decisions, it's all too easy to forget—we don't own ourselves at all. The truth is, we were bought with a price.

First of all, there's the fact that God made us. As our creator, He has every right to do with us as He pleases and to command anything of us that He pleases. We are His creation. Without Him, we wouldn't even exist.

Secondly, when we strayed from God's good and perfect will and gave ourselves over to the Devil, we condemned ourselves to an eternity of pain and suffering. But God didn't leave us helpless and hopeless. Instead, He sent His one and only Son to die for our sins—to take OUR punishment—while we were still sinners so that we could be reunited with Him. He purchased us back again, but left the choice up to us.

Imagine for a second your child was narrowly saved from a life-threatening situation by a kindhearted stranger who nearly died in the process. In your joy and appreciation, wouldn't you do anything in your power to try to make it up to that person—who saved your child when they didn't have to? Wouldn't that be the right thing to do? The truth is, God has already saved us from an eternity of pain and suffering. And He deserves our best and nothing less.

But even more than that, God deserves to be our focus and priority because of His character. God isn't just some nice, grandfatherly figure in the clouds. He's the Creator of all things visible and invisible, the author and perfecter of life itself. He is the epitome of perfection and of all things good and holy.

There are a lot of things we can worship and devote ourselves to in this life, but none deserve it more than God Himself.

Because He Commands It

"You shall have no other gods before me." — Exodus 20:3

When I tell my children to do something, I expect them to listen. In part because what I am asking of them is in their best interest, but also in part because I'm their mother and

I said so. As their mother, it is my right and responsibility to teach, guide and discipline them, and as my children, it is their responsibility to listen and obey.

It's the same way with God. As our Heavenly Father, He has the right to tell us where to go and what to do. And as His children, we have the obligation to listen. It doesn't really matter if we feel like it or not.

God has a plan that is far above and beyond anything we could ever think or imagine. We don't know all of the details, and we don't need to know all of the details. God knows what He's doing. And He expects us to listen.

So We are Available for God Appointments

God appointments are those moments when God has something special in store, either for us or for someone else, but only if we take the time to notice and participate. These moments are usually small, quiet, fleeting and incredibly easy to miss, especially when we are busy and not in tune with God's will. Tune your heart to notice them, however, and you'll be amazed to see just how often God works great miracles in even the smallest of everyday situations.

For example, when I was in college, I was a Wednesday night teacher for a fifth grade class at a small church on the bad side of town. One night, it quickly became clear that there was an issue between a couple of the girls, so we stepped out of the class for a bit to sort out whatever was going on.

That night, when I went to church, I thought it would be a regular night of teaching and doing crafts. Little did I know that, instead, I would end up ministering to two hurting girls, teaching important lessons on kindness and forgiveness, and ultimately leading one of them to Christ.

For months afterwards, I hung the craft that we did that night on my bedroom door as a reminder to always hold my plans loosely, because you just never know when God has something more amazing and far more important in store than whatever activities you had planned for the day.

I may not know what God's plan is—none of us do—but I know that I want to be a part of it. And that's never going to happen until I make myself available and willing to go wherever He asks me whenever He asks me, even if it doesn't make sense at the time.

So We Don't Miss Out On the Fullness that God Offers

I heard a story once, a long time ago, about a little girl who had a fake pearl necklace that she loved dearly. She took excellent care of it and wore it every single day.

One day, however, her father asked her to give her beloved necklace to him instead. For days, the girl resisted. She adored her necklace, and she didn't know why her father would ask her to give up something she loved so much. Every day, she told him no; she wanted to keep it.

Until one day, she finally said yes. She didn't know why her father would take away something that meant so much to her, but she decided to trust him.

That night, her father gave her a real pearl necklace that was far more beautiful and valuable than the cheap costume jewelry she'd been clinging to before. The girl was surprised and absolutely delighted.

The moral of this story is this: while there are plenty of things in our lives that we love and would never want to get rid of, the truth is that we never know just what God has in store. Ultimately, we have to trust that God loves us, that He knows what He's doing and that He wants the best for us. And when He asks us to give up something—even something good—it's only because He has something bigger and better in mind, even if we never know what it is on this side of Heaven.

To Keep Us Near to God

If we're being honest, I think most of us would admit that we're lazy. We know what we should do, but we take the easy way out instead. We don't talk to our spouses about important issues in order to avoid having to work through them. We let our children watch too much TV when we're too tired to play. We hit the drive-thru instead of cooking a homemade meal. And we do the same thing with God.

Believe it or not, going to church every Sunday is easy. Reading your Bible on a daily basis is easy. Dropping a check in the offering plate is easy. But surrendering our whole lives to God and fully embracing all that He has for us when we have no idea where it will lead? That's hard! Humbling ourselves enough to admit our biggest areas of weakness—the areas where we fall flat time and time again—to ask for help on the journey? That's hard!

But the good news is, the more we humble ourselves, place our own wants and needs aside, and make God our #1 priority, the closer we draw to Him and the more everything falls into place.

Because Life Goes that Much Better When We Do

How often do you feel stressed, worn out, exhausted or overwhelmed? While society would lead us to believe that feelings like these are simply a normal part of life, the truth is that they aren't supposed to be and they don't have to be.

"The thief comes only to steal and kill and destroy; I have come that they may have life, and have it to the full." — John 10:10

When we place God at the center of our lives, we find unexplainable joy, balance and peace. Everything begins to make sense, everything begins to fall into place and we know we have nothing to worry about. God has it all under control; we just have to listen and not mess things up.

In one of my very favorite praise and worship songs, "Our God" by Chris Tomlin, Tomlin sings *"And if our God is for us, then who could ever stop us? And if our God is for us, then what could stand against?"*

I find this song, which is based off of Romans 8:31-32, incredibly encouraging. When we center our lives around Jesus, NOTHING can stand in our way. It doesn't matter what we are up against, either—whether health issues, money issues, relationship issues or anything else. When we commit to doing things God's way, everything WILL all work out in the end—guaranteed! That's quite a promise!

This doesn't mean we'll never have problems, of course. We certainly will. But when our focus is Jesus above all else, all of those other problems simply don't matter quite as much anymore.

I don't know about you, but it seems pretty foolish to turn down a 100 percent satisfaction guaranteed promise to me—especially when God Himself is the one offering it. What could be better than that? Nothing I know of.

Chapter 4

What Does Putting God First Look Like?

When I was younger, I was fortunate enough to know several men and women who were incredibly strong in their faith. I saw firsthand how they really did put God first in their lives, even when it wasn't easy or convenient. When things went wrong, they didn't worry or complain like most of us would; they truly trusted God to take care of things. They read their Bibles and spent time in prayer because they truly enjoyed it, not because they felt they "should" or had to. They were full of joy and excited to see what God had in store for them, and it showed.

I remember looking at them with a sense of awe. What made them so different? Were they just lucky enough to be born or gifted with such incredible faith? Was it really possible to give up everything of this world to really focus on Jesus?

They never knew it, but I looked at them almost like superheroes of the faith. Surely they had something I didn't have or knew something I didn't know.

And yet, at the same time, I've always had this strange feeling that "That will be me someday." I had no idea when or how, but I've always known that eventually I would have to surrender everything and give it all over to God. In light of Christ and all He's done for us, is there really any other alternative?

Honestly, I think one obstacle that gets in the way of many Christians today is simply the fact that there is a lack of mentorship and guidance. Everywhere we turn, we find sermons, blog posts and books (like this one!) that can give us plenty of helpful tips and tricks for being more Godly, but when it comes to real, intentional relationships, they are often sorely lacking.

We know we should be more devoted to Christ, but we don't really know how. What does "putting God first" really look like in day-to-day life? How do we get to that point? What should we do when we encounter obstacles along the way?

Listen to the wrong sermons or read the wrong blog posts, articles and books and it's easy to think that certain aspects of Christianity matter far more than they really do. So before we even discuss what putting God first looks like, let's take a minute to discuss what it does not look like.

Putting God First Does NOT Mean:

• You have to be perfect.

• You can never have any fun.

• You have to pray or read your Bible for hours every day.

• You have to carry your Bible with you everywhere you go.

• You have to decorate your home with all sorts of religious icons.

• You have to wear long skirts or religious jewelry.

• You have to be involved in lots of church groups and volunteer committees.

• You have to become a missionary.

• You have to evangelize door to door.

Now, don't get me wrong. There isn't anything wrong with any of these things. They just aren't the point. You might do a few of these things because you genuinely want to and find benefit from them, but simply doing them alone is not going to make you a better Christian.

The good news is: putting God first is actually a lot more simple and straightforward than you might think.

If you are married, do you remember what it was like when you were first dating your husband? How your whole life practically revolved around him? He was the first thing you thought about every morning and the last thing you thought about every night. All throughout the day, whenever anything happened to you—whether good or bad—you couldn't wait until you had a chance to talk to him and tell him about it.

When you made decisions, such as "Should I buy this dress?" or "Should I dye my hair?" you stopped first to consider what he would think and if he would like it. When you talked to your friends, you found ways to bring him up in conversation. Just thinking about him always brought a smile to your face.

Okay, so that probably sounds pretty cheesy, but for most of us women, isn't that how it goes? When you're in love, it shows. It permeates your entire being, changes your outlook on life and affects your decisions. It's intoxicating, thrilling, exciting, breathtaking and romantic. And you can have that with God as well.

The truth is, God is already madly in love with you and deeply committed to you. He created you, He knows you inside and out, and He wants a deep and amazing relationship with you. But He's not going to force it on you. You have to decide to enter into a relationship with Him and put Him first.

Putting God First DOES Mean:

• You relentlessly seek out God's path for your life, and you do your best to stay on it.

• You do your best to make sure that in everything you do, you do it in a way that brings glory and honor to God.

• You intentionally seek to grow in your relationship with God daily.

• You begin to filter your life through a sort of "God lens" so you see things the way He would.

• You make living a God-honoring life the very core of your being or the very reason for your existence, because it is.

If these five tasks seem too lofty and unattainable, that's because they are. Not one of us is perfect, and we're always going to fall short and fall flat time and time again. But the good news is that perfection isn't required. Perfection is God's job, not yours. Your job is simply to do your best to grow and improve every single day and to trust God with the rest.

I'm not going to lie. It won't be easy and it will take a lot of time. There will be times when you will feel lazy and unmotivated. Times when you'll be angry and times when you simply can't bring yourself to care. There will be times when you think you've finally gotten it all figured out, only to realize how desperately in need of the Savior's help you are.

But this thing called Christianity, it isn't a destination or a label. It's a journey. It's a living, breathing relationship with an incredible, loving and forgiving God. And one thing I can promise you: it is worth it when you really commit to be all in, holding nothing back.

So, are you ready to make God your number one priority? The second section of this book will show you how.

<u>Section Two</u>

How to Make God the #1 Priority in Every Area of Your Life

Chapter 5

Making God a Priority in Your Daily Life

"We are as intimate with God as we choose to be." —
Cynthia Heald

If you've ever had a long-distance relationship, whether with a significant other, a friend or even a child who has gone off to college, you know how difficult it can be to remain close in heart when you're miles away. Occasional visits, phone calls and Skype sessions simply aren't the same as getting together regularly to keep in touch.

When my husband and I were first dating, there was a brief period when we went from living across town from each other to living several hours apart. The separation was temporary, but he was convinced he had lost me for good. After all, how could a relationship withstand that type of separation? Everyone knows long-distance relationships are difficult and rarely last.

And yet, how often do we voluntarily distance ourselves from God? The truth is, one distracted hour a week is simply not enough to develop a deep, long-lasting relationship, whether with God, your spouse or anyone else. If you truly want to develop a rich and fulfilling relationship with God, you need to make Him an important part of your everyday life. Here's how you can do just that.

Choose the Method that Works Best for You

According to Dr. Howard Gardner, former professor of education at Harvard University, not all people learn the same way. Instead, people generally learn best when taught according to their varying learning styles, such as visual-spatial, bodily-kinesthetic, musical or interpersonal. It only makes sense then, that when it comes to learning and growing in the Lord, we each grow a little differently.

Which situations or practices best help you grow as a Christian? Maybe you love to get out and surround yourself with nature, spending quiet time alone with God while hiking in the early morning hours. Maybe you feel closest to God when listening to meaningful old hymns or contemporary praise and worship music. Whatever helps you grow, you'll want to find a way to incorporate it into your daily life somehow.

Of course, sometimes this can be difficult to do as a busy mom with pressing family demands. That's okay; you just have to get creative. Play worship music while you do the dishes. Take the kids to the park or the library to play so you can sit and read your Bible. Put the baby in the stroller or bike seat so you can cruise around the neighborhood in peace, praying all along the way. Time with God doesn't have to consist of an hour-long prayer and Bible-reading block first thing in the morning. Find whatever works best for your personality and your life.

...But Don't Forget the Classics

Of course, while it is important to seek God in the way you most enjoy or get the most out of, that doesn't mean that you can neglect the most important spiritual disciplines just because you find them less desirable, enjoyable or convenient. Practices such as attending church regularly, reading the Bible and praying are always going to be important, no matter how you feel about them or how difficult it is to fit them in.

If you don't enjoy participating in spiritual disciplines like attending church, reading the Bible or praying, you might want to ask yourself why as well as what you can do about it. Do you need to find a different church or purchase a different translation of the Bible? Do you have hang-ups over prayer that you need to address? Could you use a certain prayer formula or even certain, pre-written prayers to help make prayer easier for you? Do you need to switch your schedule around to be more accommodating or lower your expectations of yourself? There is a reason these disciplines are staple practices of the Christian faithful. Don't neglect them.

Start Small

If you aren't already in the habit of spending quiet time with God, it's unrealistic to expect yourself to suddenly be able to sit down and pray or read your Bible for an hour straight. Just like running a marathon, you have to build up your stamina gradually.

If five minutes of prayer is all you can manage the first day, that's okay! It's five more than you spent the day before. Aim to gradually increase your time as you can, and it won't be long until your quiet times seem to fly right by.

Don't get caught up in the numbers game, though. It's not the amount of time that matters. God's not up in Heaven keeping track of your quiet times on a scorecard. There's no prize for the most minutes completed each month, and if you focus on the numbers alone, you'll completely miss the point.

Instead, simply aim to make your quiet times meaningful and enjoyable, even if they are short. As you get into the habit and routine, you'll naturally start to look forward to them more and more each day, and that's where true growth will happen.

Find Accountability

Are you having trouble motivating yourself to spend time with God every day? You definitely aren't alone. Oftentimes, the hardest part of creating new habits is simply getting started. Thankfully, having someone to hold you accountable can really help.

Ask your spouse, a friend, or even create a small group of people to check in with you regularly to see how you're doing. Print out a calendar to use as a checklist or create a Bible-reading schedule to keep you on track. You can even use a free app, such as MakeMe, to motivate yourself until you get into the habit. Create goals or motivate yourself with a reward—whatever it takes. While you probably won't want or need to rely on these strategies long term, they can provide just the motivation you need to get started.

Be Willing to Adjust as Needed

Lastly, don't be afraid to adjust as needed. There will be times in your life when you are more busy and times when you are less busy, and trying to keep the exact same quiet time schedule no matter what life throws your way is a great way to drive yourself crazy.

Last winter I used to have regular quiet times with God over lunch. With my husband at work, my oldest at school and my youngest fast asleep, lunchtime was the one time of day that I knew I could enjoy interruption free. Once summer time came around, my oldest wasn't in school and my youngest's naptime shifted into the afternoons, I moved my quiet times to late at night after everyone had gone to bed. There's no magic time or formula. Choose the time you are most likely to follow through with, and don't be afraid to move it around as needed.

Each and every one of us has the same 24 hours in a day, and it's up to each of us to decide how we use them. Will you use your week to bring honor and glory to God and to further develop a strong, Christian faith that will carry you through anything? Or will you fritter it away with nothing of any consequence to show for it?

Making God the number one priority in your daily life doesn't mean that you have to spend your entire day attending church, reading the Bible or volunteering for a worthy cause to the point where you have no time left for anything else. Instead, simply honor God wherever you are. Make Him your focus and your priority, and everything else will fall into place.

Chapter 6

Making God a Priority in Your Marriage

"Though one may be overpowered, two can defend themselves. A cord of three strands is not quickly broken." — *Ecclesiastes 4:12*

Of all of the relationships you'll have during your adult life, your relationship with your spouse is arguably the most important (other than your relationship with God, of course!). For better or for worse, no other individual will impact you, shape you and affect your life the way your spouse will.

That's why making God a priority in your marriage is so important. Center your marriage around God, and you can create a rock-solid marriage that will form the basis for a God-centered, joy-filled, missional life. Center your marriage on your own selfish needs and desires, and you are far more likely to experience dissatisfaction, discontentment and trials of all kinds.

Of course, I'm certainly not saying that only Christians can have happy marriages. But knowing how difficult marriage can be sometimes, I'd really rather not do it without the extra help!

After all, I don't want just your average, ordinary, run-of-the-mill marriage. I want an incredible marriage that sets the foundation for a incredible life and an incredible ministry. Do you long for the same? Here's how you can make that happen.

Find Your Purpose

Chances are, before you got married, you thought long and hard to make sure that the person you were marrying was the right person for you. After all, no one wants to wake up one morning only to realize that they made a terrible mistake. One question you may not have thought to ask yourself, however, was, "Why am I getting married in the first place?"

Most people get married because they love the other person and can't imagine their lives without them or because the other person makes them happy. While these things are nice, they simply aren't enough. If you want a truly remarkable marriage that is everything God wants you to have, you need to set your sights much, much higher, and a marriage mission statement can help you do just that.

Creating a marriage mission statement may sound complicated, but it is actually way easier than it sounds. Simply talk with your spouse about what you would like to accomplish with your marriage and go to the Lord together in prayer to see what big plans He might have in store for you.

Every couple's marriage statement will be different, but here are a few examples to get you thinking:

• To provide a positive example for our friends and family members

• To encourage those in difficult relationships to stick it out

• To provide a strong and stable home in which to raise Godly children

• To support and encourage each other as we fulfill God's callings in our lives

Falling into lazy and ineffective habits and patterns is all too easy to do, even in the best of marriages. With a marriage mission statement in place, you and your husband can intentionally choose to work together to order your life toward the things that matter most.

Model Your Love After Christ's Love

I hate to break it to you, but much of what you've learned about love is probably wrong, especially if you've been taking your cues from the entertainment industry. The world will tell you that your ideal partner is someone who makes you happy. That if your spouse isn't treating you like a queen, you shouldn't put up with it. That life is too short to spend with the wrong person, and that divorce is no big deal.

Now, yes, you should want happiness in marriage, there are times when you may need to stand up for yourself, and there are even times when divorce is warranted, but the truth is, if you follow the advice of the world, you're going to end up with a worldly marriage and nothing more.

Instead, take a look at what the Bible has to say about marriage. In Ephesians 5, Paul writes that marriage is designed to mirror Christ's relationship with the church. And how does Christ regard the church? We can see more about this in the famous love chapter, 1 Corinthians 13.

"Love is patient, love is kind. It does not envy, it does not boast, it is not proud. It does not dishonor others, it is not self-seeking, it is not easily angered, it keeps no record of wrongs. Love does not delight in evil but rejoices with the truth. It always protects, always trusts, always hopes, always perseveres. Love never fails." —1 Corinthians 13:4-8a

Try substituting your name in for the word "love." Does this passage describe the way you treat your spouse? *"I am patient, I am kind. I do not envy, I do not boast, I am not proud..."* If not, you may have some work to do! (And if we're being honest, all of us do!) It's a long list, but the better you get at it, the more wonderful and God-centered your marriage will be.

Put Each Other in Your Rightful Places

The media loves to portray husbands as bumbling idiots. Thankfully, for most of us, nothing could be further from the truth! Many of us have amazing husbands who do their best every day to lead and provide for our families as best as they know how. And yet, how often do we treat our husbands with disrespect, indifference or even scorn—often without even realizing it?

Your husband is a dearly beloved child of God. He is valuable and important to God, and he deserves to be treated that way. Do you treat your husband as the man of God that he is, or do you treat him like an inferior partner or even a child? Do you ever criticize him, insult him, embarrass him or disregard him? Do you ever stand in his way or in his place to prevent him from being the man God created him to be?

God gave your husband to you as a gift for your mutual edification. His job is to lift you up and to lead you toward God and greater holiness, and your job is to do the same for him. Your job isn't to make each other happy or to solve each other's problems. It's to love and serve each other and to use that love to help and serve others as well.

Share Your Struggles

While just the thought of sharing your struggles with your spouse might leave you feeling terrified, vulnerable and exposed, actually opening up and sharing your struggles might be the best thing that you can do for your marriage. Not only does sharing your struggles allow you to grow closer as a couple, but it also allows you to minister to each other and to help each other overcome any obstacles the two of you may currently be facing.

Whether your struggles are spiritual, financial, health-related or something else, don't try to carry your burdens alone. Lean on each other and go to God together in prayer. That's what marriage is for, and you'll both be stronger because of it.

Pray

How often do you pray specifically for your husband and for your marriage? And even more importantly than that, how often do you pray together?

Prayer is powerful. It can turn a lifeless marriage into a thriving one, an impossible situation into a beautiful one and a cold heart into an open one. And it isn't just your prayers themselves that are powerful. Prayer doesn't just allow God to act; simply the act of praying will change you as well.

As you and your husband pray together, you'll begin to open up to each other and share from a deeper level. You'll learn to lean on each other and on God. You'll learn how you can better support each other no matter what are going through. You'll grow closer to God and to each other, and you'll begin to unlock all that God has for you in your marriage.

After all, Christianity isn't meant to be an independent journey. As husband and wife, you are in the unique position to help each other draw closer to God in a way that no one else can. Pray for each other and with each other. Share your struggles, fears, concerns and joys. Hold each other accountable. You'll both be stronger for it, and it will help those around you be stronger in their marriages as well, even if you don't realize it.

Chapter 7

Making God a Priority in Your Parenting

"Start children off on the way they should go, and even when they are old they will not turn from it." —Proverbs 22:6

According to research done by Kara E. Powell and Chap Clark and compiled into the book "Sticky Faith: Everyday Ideas to Build Lasting Faith in Your Kids," approximately 60 percent of high school students walk away from the faith around the time they enter college, and many never return. Clearly, raising children in a Christian home simply isn't enough.

Instead, if we want to raise children who fully embrace the faith and choose to continue to do so after they are out of the house, we need to equip them to do so. This means equipping ourselves to be the Godly parents they need, preparing them for the real world and imparting to them a faith that is strong enough to last through any trials or tribulations they may face. Here's how to do just that.

Understand that Your Children are Not Your Own

With a school-aged child, a toddler and one on the way, I can tell you with certainty that it doesn't take long for your children to feel like your own. You love them, care for them and are responsible for them. And yet, the truth is that your children aren't really your own at all. Instead, they are

God's children whom He has graciously given to you to teach, guide and take care of.

As the caretaker of God's children, you are not only expected to take good care of them, but someday you will be held accountable for the job that you did. Did you diligently lead them toward Him every day? Or did you simply keep them alive until they were out of the house? Perfection is absolutely not required, but you do have an obligation to give it your best effort.

Improve Your Own Walk

Your children depend on you to show them what it means to be a committed Christian. If you aren't a committed Christian yourself, not only will you not know how or what to teach them, but you won't be able to teach them effectively, as raising Godly children often takes more than we, as humans, can manage ourselves.

If you've been lackadaisical with your own faith up until this point, raising Godly children can provide a good source of motivation to be the kind of committed Christian you want your children to have as an example. I know, personally, on days when I don't feel like going to church or taking the time to say nighttime prayers with my children before I tuck them into bed, I remember that if I make it optional for me, I'm sending the message that it's unimportant or optional for them as well. And that's usually just the motivation I need.

Seek Guidance and Direction

When I was pregnant with my oldest son, I read pretty much every single baby and parenting book I could get my hands on. I wanted to be prepared from the start, and I believe that all of this reading and learning has served me well. Not only am I better able to parent my own children, but I am also frequently able to help other mothers who come to me for advice, both online and in real life.

Unfortunately, however, simply stocking up on knowledge beforehand isn't enough. Not only is it impossible to remember everything you've read, but sometimes you'll find yourself in a situation you didn't anticipate or you'll find that the methods you've read about previously simply aren't a good fit for your child or your family.

This is why it is important to continually seek guidance and direction from trusted and reliable sources. Not only should you frequently go to the Lord in prayer, but you also need a network of Godly friends (preferably with children of various ages) as well as access to plenty of books, articles and podcasts. Trust me, you'll need them!

Teach Your Children Christian Disciplines

Want to raise children who pray fervently, read their Bibles voraciously, memorize Scripture regularly and attend church gladly? Then you'll want to start these habits at home from an early age. Children can begin learning basic prayers from about the time they start talking, and they can enjoy listening to stories in a children's Bible from the time they are born.

The first prayer my sons learned was just a simple *"Thank you, Jesus, for [fill in the blank]. Amen."* Now that my oldest son is a bit bigger, he's currently working on more complicated prayers such as the "Our Father" and the "Glory Be." We also say prayers when we pass a car crash, when my son Is scared at bedtime or when someone in our family is having a particularly grouchy day.

Keep in mind, if your children aren't excited about these disciplines at first, that's completely normal and perfectly okay. It's a learning process. Keep the learning process lighthearted, simple and enjoyable, and as your children grow up, these practices will hopefully turn into treasured habits that they'll carry with them always.

Impart a Real Faith

Of course, while Christian disciplines are incredibly important, disciplines and rituals are simply tools for growth, not the end result themselves. One of the quickest ways to impart a shallow and lifeless faith to your children is to teach them all the rules and regulations without also taking the time to help them develop a real relationship and a strong belief system that can stand the test of time.

Teach your children the rules, but don't stop there. Teach them *why*. Give them guidelines, and give them the knowledge they need to make decisions when you aren't around. Give them a set of values and morals, not just do's and don'ts.

Real faith sometimes questions, falters and makes mistakes. If your children do the same, that's okay! Questioning doesn't mean your children are falling away; it means they are processing what they have learned to hopefully make their faith their own. Making mistakes doesn't mean they are doomed to a lifetime of sin; it simply means they are learning.

Your job isn't to make sure they do everything just right. It's to guide and support them as they learn, make mistakes and discover a real, lasting faith they can truly call their own.

Model the Spiritual Life You Want Your Children to Have

No matter how diligent you are about teaching your children right from wrong, the truth is that the majority of the lessons they learn from you will be the ones you teach without meaning to. Whether you worry about your weight, have a temper in the car or always have to have the latest and greatest tech gadgets, your children probably will too.

Therefore, if you want to raise Godly children, you have to model what Godliness looks like day in and day out. Do you make God a priority in your own life? How do you react when you are worried, stressed, frustrated or joyful? Do you go out of your way to help others, or are you constantly trying to upgrade your own life instead? Chances are, your children will grow up to act the same way.

Being a parent is a privilege that comes with a lot of great perks, but it also comes with a great deal of responsibility as well. As a mother, you have the power to significantly impact the next generation and even to change the entire world. It's hard, but it's so, so worth it.

Chapter 8

Making God a Priority in Your Home

"The Lord's curse is on the house of the wicked, but he blesses the home of the righteous." — *Proverbs 3:33*

Your home is your home base. It's the place where you rest, relax and rejuvenate, the place where you teach your children and the place where you develop a closer relationship with your spouse. Make God a priority in your home, and you'll make Him a priority in your life as well.

After all, God doesn't just dwell in church for one hour on Sunday mornings. You can invite Him into your home to share in your everyday life as well. Whether you're spending time with the family on a relaxed Saturday morning, entertaining guests on a fun-filled Friday night or doing the dishes while helping your children with their math homework on a Tuesday afternoon, you can (and should!) give God a prominent place in your home as well. Here's how.

Create an Atmosphere of Peace and Love

If your home is chaotic, the rest of your life probably will be too. Instead, create an atmosphere of peace and love. You can do this by taking care of yourself physically, keeping your schedules simple, creating routines, incorporating fun and play into your daily life and keeping your home neat and tidy. Keeping your home clean and clutter-free may not sound all that spiritual, but honestly, having a tidy home can make a huge difference in your family's spiritual life as well.

If your daily life is full of bad habits or destructive patterns, find ways to get rid of them. Turn off the TV so you can really pay attention to each other. Yell less and guide more. Designate a specific spot for your keys so you aren't getting upset looking for them all of the time. Anything you can do to make your home life go more smoothly is worth the time investment.

Be Hospitable

Our home may be on the small side, but I absolutely love having people over as much as possible. After all, what better way is there to walk beside people, witness to them and encourage them than to regularly invite them into your home and do life with them?

While it is certainly okay to enjoy times of peace and quiet with just your family, if your home only ever has your family in it, you are missing out on a wonderful ministry opportunity.

Your get-togethers don't have to be elaborate to be impactful. Invite your children's friends over for a sleepover. Invite your husband's friends over to watch the game. Have your girlfriends over for an impromptu brunch. Invite friends and co-workers who don't have family nearby to join you for the holidays. The more the merrier.

Remove Distractions

What things around your home distract you or prevent you from spending as much time with God as you'd like? Do you stay up too late playing on the computer or watching TV or movies? Do you have so much housework that you struggle to keep up? What do you do when you should be spending time with God? Take some time to identify these distractions.

Next, find ways to remove or reduce them. For example, you might cancel your cable subscription, keep all electronics out of the bedroom or give away half of your movie collection. You might commit to spend the next four weeks massively decluttering and organizing your home so cleaning up takes less time. Whatever is getting in the way of your relationship with God, get rid of it. You don't need it.

Place Objects Around Your Home as Reminders

Want to keep God firmly in the front and center of your mind? Place objects around your house to remind you to pray, read your Bible or spend time with Him. There are literally tons of ways you can do this; feel free to pick the ones that work best for you!

• Leave your Bible in the bathroom, on your bedside table, in your purse or next to your favorite chair so it's always nearby when you have a few extra minutes to read it.

• Place scriptures around your home where you're sure to see them.

• Hang a rosary or other religious item on your mirror or from a lamp, or place it on your bedside table.

• Hang a cross or crucifix on your wall where you'll see it regularly.

Create a Special Quiet Space

It can also be helpful to dedicate a specific space in your home as a special quiet time space. It doesn't have to be big or elaborate; simply having a space where you always spend time with the Lord in prayer will help you focus every time you're there.

Choose a spot where you are unlikely to be distracted, such as a bench in the backyard, an armchair in the guest room or even the kitchen table while your children are in school. Keep anything you may need in a basket nearby, such as your Bible, journal, pens, prayer list, rosary beads, praise and worship music, or whatever you like. Then, every time you visit this space, you'll be ready to focus, learn, listen and grow.

Your home is your sanctuary; make it God's sanctuary too. Then, no matter where God leads you once you step foot outside of your front door, you'll be ready to honor God and put Him first in all you do. After all, you're already in the habit.

Chapter 9

Making God a Priority in the Workplace

"Whatever you do, work at it with all your heart, as working for the Lord, not for human masters, since you know that you will receive an inheritance from the Lord as a reward. It is the Lord Christ you are serving." — Colossians 3:23-24

Putting God first on a Sunday generally isn't too difficult. Between church in the morning, a special Sunday dinner and an afternoon perfect for napping, restful Sundays are one habit that is pretty easy to fall into. What happens when Monday morning rolls around, however?

If you're like most people, you segment your days into certain categories. Sunday is for church. Monday through Friday are for work. Saturday is for errands and activities with the kids. What if God doesn't want to be confined to just one day a week, however?

If you work outside of the home (or even if you work from the home), work probably takes up a significant portion of your time, and how you spend this time matters. Work isn't just for bringing in a paycheck to cover your bills. It's also another very important avenue for putting God first, living out your full potential in Christ and being a witness to those around you. Here's how you can do just that.

Greet Every Day with Joy and Gratitude

When you walk into work each morning, what is your typical attitude like? Are you irritable and miserable to be around, or are you truly joyful and excited about the opportunity to serve God for another day?

It doesn't really matter how you feel about your job. As a Christian, you are Christ's ambassador to the world, and the way you respond to your day-to-day challenges will shape how the nonbelievers around you perceive both God and Christianity as a whole. Are you setting a good example?

Refuse to Participate in Ungodly Activities

Unless you work in a church (and sometimes probably even then), chances are you will regularly face situations in which your ethics will be put to the test. Your boss might ask you to lie to a customer, your coworkers might try to engage you in office gossip, or you might be tempted to fudge a few numbers to make your department look better.

Doing the right thing, even when it's hard, isn't always easy or popular, but it's the only way to put God first. And honestly, what's more important—your faith or the compromising situation you find yourself in? Your faith will last you an eternity. The situation you're in right now will be over before you know it. Make your decisions with eternity in mind.

Develop Real, Intentional Relationships

Work is a great place to develop relationships with a wide variety of people, many of whom you might not connect with otherwise. While it may be tempting to stick to yourself or stay close to those who believe the same things you do, go out on a limb and develop real, intentional relationships with all sorts of people, including those who you maybe don't have as much in common with.

Doing so is beneficial for a few reasons. Not only does having a variety of friends make life richer and more interesting, but it's also the best way to minister and share the Gospel with those around you who don't already believe.

No one wants to be preached to by someone they don't know. Develop a close friendship with someone, however, and when they have a tough time, they will naturally come to you for advice. This is the perfect time to share what you believe and encourage the other person without coming across as preachy, arrogant or self-righteous.

Talk About God When Appropriate

While many people think of sharing the good news of Jesus's death and resurrection as THE way to share the Gospel, the fact is that overt faith-based conversations are only a small part of our mission here on Earth. If you launch straight into *"Hi, I'm Brittany. Do you know about Jesus??"* the first time you meet people, you'll probably come across as a crazy person and ruin your chances of sharing with them in the future.

The truth is, laying out the plan for salvation may be the most important conversation you could ever have, but it's only one conversation out of many, and it isn't appropriate until the time is right.

Instead, find ways to talk about everyday life in a casual manner between friends. Let your faith be the basis, not necessarily the topic, of your conversations, especially if the person isn't ready or interested in listening to the Gospel right now. You certainly don't have to (and shouldn't) hide the fact that you are a Christian, but there's no need to shove it down their throats either.

Talk about current events, your kids and your weekend plans. Discuss your struggles and achievements and get to know theirs. Build real, solid friendships because you genuinely like them, not just because you want to convert them. They are a person, not a project. Then, when the topic of Christianity does come up, you can share within the context of a solid, caring friendship, not as a crazy person on a soapbox.

Whether you work four hours a week or forty, if you are called to work outside the home, you are also called to use this opportunity to the glory and honor of God. Don't just show up, do your job and collect your paycheck. Treat it as a platform and a mission field, and you may just be amazed at how your perspective on work changes as a result.

Chapter 10

Making God a Priority in Your Finances

"'Bring the whole tithe into the storehouse, that there may be food in my house. Test me in this,' says the Lord Almighty, 'and see if I will not throw open the floodgates of heaven and pour out so much blessing that there will not be room enough to store it.'" — Malachi 3:10

According to an article in Relevant Magazine, only five percent of the U.S. tithes. Among Christians, the average tithe is only 2.5 percent per capita, despite the fact that many believers would still consider 10 percent (or more) to be the ideal standard giving rate. According to an article on ChristianityToday.com, only 10 to 25 percent of church-goers tithe on average, and this small portion makes up 50 to 80 percent of church funding.

If these statistics make you feel better about your haphazard giving, these next ones won't. Apparently, if every believer regularly tithed 10 percent of their income, the church could end global hunger, eliminate deaths from preventable diseases, end illiteracy, solve world water and sanitation issues, fully fund overseas missions work AND expand their ministries both at home and abroad. And yet, we don't give.

The problem isn't that we don't have enough money. Tithing rates were higher during the Great Depression than they are now. The problem is that we aren't putting God first in our money, and the world is paying the price for it.

Change Your Perspective

From Psalm 24:1, which states *"The earth is the Lord's, and everything in it, the world, and all who live in it"* to Psalm 50:10, which states *"for every animal of the forest is mine, and the cattle on a thousand hills,"* the Bible makes it pretty clear that our money is not actually our own, but God's.

It doesn't matter how much or how little you have, how much you spend or save, or how long and hard you've worked to achieve the balance in your bank account—it's all God's anyways. It isn't ours, and we don't get to keep it. Instead, our role is simply to faithfully manage what we are given. And someday, we will be asked to give an account for it.

When you fully realize and accept this fact, it will change the way you look at money forever. Instead of asking, "What do I want to buy?" "What can I afford?" or "How should I invest my money?" you start asking questions like "What would God want me to do with this money?" and "How can I use the money I have to further the kingdom today?" In short, it changes everything.

Examine Your Motives

Well-known pastor Francis Chan once shared in a sermon how frustrated he was with rich people who said they were Christians and had so much ability to give generously and then simply didn't. He shared how he prayed out of frustration, "God, make me rich, then!" And God did.

Chan's book, "Crazy Love," has sold millions of copies, generating millions of dollars worth of income, making Chan one rich pastor. Chan hasn't kept the money for himself, however. Instead, approximately 90 percent of all of Chan's income goes straight to charity while Chan continues to live the same modest lifestyle he's always had. His wife even sold her wedding ring in order to be able to give more generously. That's commitment.

Tons of people pray this same prayer every year: "God, make me rich!" And yet, for most people, this overnight financial success simply doesn't happen. How did Chan get so lucky?

While it's impossible to speak of God's motives for sure, the outcome only makes sense. If you were a business owner looking for someone to manage your assets, who would you entrust your money to? The one who would squander it all on a nicer house, a nicer car, fancy vacations and a wardrobe full of clothes for themselves? Or the one who would take that money and use it to accomplish your mission here on earth?

I doubt there is a single one of us who would object to a big pay increase, but honestly, what's the point? So you can have nicer stuff? If you aren't serving God with the little you have now, chances are that isn't going to change if you had more.

Whether you are steeped in debt or living with plenty, the question you should be asking yourself isn't "How can I pay off my debt faster?" or "How can I increase my income?" but "How can I honor God with His money today?"

Not that you can never pay off your debt or have nice things—those things just shouldn't be the point. The point of money (and everything else in life) is to glorify God, not just to acquire more stuff you don't even need anyways. And when you learn how to do that, you may just find that you had more than enough all along.

Give Cheerfully

Several years ago, the pastor of the church I was attending at the time gave a sermon on being a cheerful giver, based on 1 Corinthians 9:7. For weeks afterwards, the congregation would burst into loud and vigorous applause every time the offering plate was passed. It was pretty awesome. Even now, six years later, you can still hear a few people clapping loudly at that point in the service.

What if—instead of viewing giving as an annoying or guilt-inducing obligation or duty—we saw it for what it really is? Giving should never be just another bill to pay or check to write when we're feeling okay on money. Instead, it should be a celebration of all we've been given, a chance to grow closer to God and to deepen our faith and a chance to help others and to live out the Gospel.

Do you have a car? If so, you are wealthier than 92 percent of the world's population, according to Compassion International. Do you have Internet at home? If so, you are richer than 97 percent of the world's population. No matter how broke we all may feel at times, the truth is that we are truly blessed with an absolute abundance far beyond what we really need. It's only natural then, that we should want to use this abundance to help those who are less fortunate.

If you'd love to be able to put God first in your finances, but you simply don't know how you can possibly manage it and the sheer thought of trying to do so gives you anxiety, let me just say, I've been there! Putting God first in your finances can be scary. But it can also be incredibly rewarding, not just financially but spiritually as well.

Every time I've laid myself aside and put God first in the way I use the money He has given me, He always, always comes through. It may not be right away or in a huge and noticeable way—after all, He isn't just a giant ATM in the sky—but He does come through. Trust Him in this—even if it's only a little at first—and then sit back and see what He will do. You might just be amazed at what happens when you give God the chance to work.

Chapter 11

Making God a Priority in Your Friendships

"And let us consider how we may spur one another on toward love and good deeds, not giving up meeting together, as some are in the habit of doing, but encouraging one another—and all the more as you see the Day approaching." — Hebrews 10:24-25

If you're like most people, you probably chose your friends pretty haphazardly. Whether you are blessed with just a few friends or lots, most of them are probably people you met randomly through work, church, mom's groups, or your children's activities. You didn't go out specifically looking for certain types of people to be friends with. Instead, your friendships probably developed fairly naturally and effortlessly over time.

For this reason, it's easy to let your friendships become lackadaisical. You get together whenever it's convenient, spend time doing whatever activity is at hand and then continue on your merry way. You don't put a great deal of thought into their friendships. You just let them happen organically.

What if we completely changed how we viewed our friendships, however? What if—instead of seeing them just as fun ways to spend our time—we started approaching them with purpose and intentionality? After all, there is no better way to really minister to others and to allow yourself to be ministered to as well than in the context of real, intentional, long-lasting friendships.

If you're ready to truly make God a priority in your life and to let Him use you to accomplish His purpose and will, making Him a priority in your friendships is a great way to do just that. Here's how you can.

Surround Yourself with the Right People

According to entrepreneur and motivational speaker Jim Rohn, *"You are the average of the five people you spend the most time with."* The Bible agrees. Proverbs 13:20 states, *"Whoever walks with the wise becomes wise, but the companion of fools will suffer harm."* Our friends have a huge impact on our spiritual lives, and we need to choose them carefully!

Think about the people you spend the most time with. Do they encourage you, build you up and push you be a better person, or do they always bring you down with their constant negativity and inappropriate behaviors? Do they set a positive example that makes you strive for more out of life, or do they encourage you to partake in unhealthy and harmful activities and behaviors?

If the people you spend the most time with are having a negative effect on your life or are leading lives that you don't want to pursue and encouraging you to do the same, it may be time to replace them with new friends who will encourage you to head in a new direction.

This doesn't mean that all of your friends should be Christians just like you, however. It is also incredibly important to develop real friendships with nonbelievers too. Personally, I have nonbelieving friends who lift me up, call me out and keep me in line more than my Christian friends do. You just have to make sure that no matter who you surround yourself with, the results are positive.

Develop Real Relationships

As an introvert, I know just how easy it is to keep people at a superficial level. Not only is too much connecting very tiring for me, but add in the fact that I pretty much always have two very energetic little boys in tow, and trust me—I know just how easy it is to keep all conversations shallow and polite.

If you want to develop intentional, Godly relationships, however, you need to dig in deeper. Share your life and listen to theirs. Share your worries, your fears, your joys and your triumphs. Be real, raw, honest and authentic. Laugh together. Cry together. Pray together.

Too many people think that, in order to make a difference, you have to have all of the answers, be able to write large checks or have experience in whatever area people are struggling in. Thankfully, nothing could be further from the truth. Sometimes, all it takes is simply the willingness to walk beside people no matter what they are going through, even if you don't know what to say or do.

Refuse to Participate in Ungodly Behavior

Depending on who your friends are, there may be times when they want to do things that you know you really should avoid. Whether it's seeing the latest questionable movie, indulging in gossip or telling little white lies to your husbands, chances are, you'll have plenty of opportunities to participate in less-than-desirable behavior.

Don't do it.

Sometimes, we can make the biggest impact simply by what we won't do, rather than by what we do. This doesn't mean that we have to lecture our friends who should know better or make a big deal out of it, of course. But by standing firm in our convictions, we make a statement and we empower our friends to do the same.

Just because your friendships are fun and enjoyable doesn't mean that they can't be intentional too. Whether your friends are Christians or not, putting God first in the way you approach your friendships can make a significant, positive difference, both in your life and in theirs.

Chapter 12

Making God a Priority in Your Entertainment

"And whatever you do, in word or deed, do everything in the name of the Lord Jesus, giving thanks to God the Father through him." — Colossians 3:17

According to data provided by the Bureau of Labor Statistics, Americans get an average of five hours of sports and leisure time on a daily basis. Of these five hours, just over half of it is spent watching TV. The rest is divided up between activities such as socializing, playing video games, reading, participating in sports and doing nothing.

While many of us often feel as though we simply do not have enough time in the day, the truth is that the vast majority of us do have several hours a week that we can choose to use as we see fit. We just spend the majority of them doing mindless activities without even really thinking about it.

What if—instead of wasting this time—we used it intentionally and purposefully? Making the most of your downtime and entertainment doesn't have to mean that you never have any fun. Instead, it simply means that you choose which types of entertainment you will and will not participate in with your priorities in mind. Here's how you can do just that.

Choose the Right Types of Entertainment

Whether you have thirty minutes to yourself or three hours, how do you spend them? What are your favorite activities to do with your friends and family on the weekends? The fact is, you have a great deal of flexibility in how you choose to spend your time, and the choice you make matters.

Do you mindlessly plop in front of the TV and watch hours of shows glorifying sex, drugs and violence? Do you scroll through Pinterest or Facebook, growing increasingly discontent with your life as you see all of the nice things everyone else has but you? Do you go out on the town with friends whose lifestyles don't match up with what you know God wants for you?

While these types of activities may seem harmless or "not that bad" at first, engaging in them over time can really take a toll on you mentally, emotionally and spiritually. Choose edifying activities that allow you to truly rest and grow instead.

Choose the Right Amount of Entertainment

Unfortunately, evaluating the types of entertainment you participate in is only the first step; you also need to take a hard look at the amount of time you spend on each of these activities. After all, activities that would be fine to engage in otherwise can quickly become a problem when they take up too much of your life.

Do you ever get so absorbed in the phone, computer or TV that you don't give your children the attention that they deserve and then snap at them when they try to get it? Do you ever stay up so late watching TV or hanging out with friends that it negatively affects your parenting or performance at work in the morning? Do you ever miss church or neglect to read your Bible or pray because you're too tired, you're behind on housework or you'd rather do other things?

While social media, television and spending time with friends can be a very positive, relaxing and enjoyable part of life, they can also easily become nothing more than a huge distraction if you aren't careful to set clear boundaries.

Evaluate How Your Choice of Entertainment Affects Yourself and Others

So, how do you know if your choice of entertainment or the amount of time you spend on your entertainment is a problem? While I think most of us know in our hearts when there is a problem, if you aren't sure, take an honest look at how your choice of entertainment is affecting your life and the lives of those around you. Ask yourself:

• Is my relationship with God as strong as it should be? If not, what is getting in the way?

• Do I look forward to times with God, approach them with dread or simply not care?

• Does my choice of entertainment build me up or tear me down? How do I feel after participating in these activities? How do I feel the next day?

• How does my choice of entertainment affect those around me? Am I spending as much time with my family and friends as I should be?

• Am I actively involved in my church, in my community or in missions work of some kind?

At the end of a long day or a long week, you should look forward to some downtime to rest, relax and rejuvenate. Even Jesus snuck away to be alone, pray and find some peace; you should too.

That doesn't mean you should just mindlessly collapse on the couch for hours every week, though. Being intentional with your entertainment may seem tiring at first, but when you order your entire life to put God first, including your entertainment, you're sure to reap the benefits later.

Chapter 13

Making God a Priority in Times of Great Trial

"Consider it pure joy, my brothers and sisters, whenever you face trials of many kinds, because you know that the testing of your faith produces perseverance. Let perseverance finish its work so that you may be mature and complete, not lacking anything." — James 1:2-4

One of the hardest questions to answer as a Christian is "Why Does God Allow Suffering?" After all, it's often difficult to understand how a God who is supposed to be so good and loving could ever allow such bad things to happen. And yet, when conducting the 2015 Equipping Godly Women reader survey, several people answered that it was exactly these times of great grief and trial that helped them grow in their faith and in their relationship with God the most.

Trials and tribulations don't have to be bad. In fact, James 1:2 says we should consider trials "pure joy!" While joy may be the last thing on your mind when you are going through a particularly rough time, the good news is that God can use your trials for good, and you can use your trials for His glory. Here's how.

Draw Near to God

A few months back, my husband and I received some troubling news. The ultrasound technician had noticed some suspicious spots on our routine prenatal ultrasound, and while they were probably nothing, they could be an indication that our unborn child had a serious chromosomal disorder that would change all of our lives forever.

We decided to have further testing done immediately, just to ease our minds, but we wouldn't have the results back for 7-10 business days. It was a tense couple of weeks until we finally got the call we'd been waiting for—the test had come back negative. Our baby has a low risk of being born with this particular problem.

Talking to my husband later that night, he shared with me how worried he had been waiting for the results. I asked him, "How much have you prayed over the last couple of weeks?" "Nonstop!" he replied.

The fact is, we will always have trials and troubles to overcome. Whether it is something as small as an unexpected bill or as serious as losing a beloved family member before their time, life will inevitably throw tons of garbage our way.

When it does, however, we have a choice. We can sit and wallow in it, or we can use it as an opportunity to draw near to God and deepen our faith. The situation may not change, but we can change ourselves to make the most of the situation and to give God the proper honor He deserves.

Reevaluate Your Priorities

Nothing will make you reevaluate your priorities quite like a tragedy. It's during times like these that we often can't help but stop, reevaluate and figure out what matters most. You shouldn't wait until tragedy strikes before you take some time to really evaluate your life, however. Times of great trial can also provide the perfect opportunity to stop and reflect.

Are you really making God your number one priority, or are you a Christian in name only? Are you surrounded by friends, family and acquaintances that build you up, or do you have toxic friendships you need to let go? Have you been the best wife, mother and friend that you can, or have you been self-centered and lazy?

When everything seems like it is falling apart, that's the perfect time to turn to God. Put your life back together His way, and you'll likely find your new life is much, much stronger than it ever could have been before.

Reach Out to Others with Similar Hurts

No matter what you are going through, whether it is a messy divorce, the death of a child, the loss of a close friendship or a devastating diagnosis, you aren't alone. Not only is God right there with you every step of the way, but you likely also have the love and support of others who are going through the exact same thing, whether in real life or online.

You owe it to yourself and to them to reach out. Not only will sharing your struggles with a friend help your healing process, but these intentional relationships can even help your friends through their own healing processes as well.

Tragedies and trials may be an inescapable part of this fallen world we live in, but that doesn't mean you have to let them define you. Use your past and current pains to minister to others going through the same things and turn your trials into great victory. You may just be surprised at what God can do when you give your hurts over to Him.

<u>Conclusion</u>

The Cost of Making God Your #1 Priority

"But whatever were gains to me I now consider loss for the sake of Christ. What is more, I consider everything a loss because of the surpassing worth of knowing Christ Jesus my Lord, for whose sake I have lost all things. I consider them garbage, that I may gain Christ" — Philippians 3:7-8

I'm not going to lie. Making God the number one priority in every area of your life isn't easy, and you'll never be able to attain perfection. Just like the story of the little girl with the pearl necklace I mentioned in chapter three, you will likely have to give up things—even things you love or that are important to you—in order to exchange them for something far more valuable.

There will be times when you'll get angry, when you'll feel selfish and when you won't be able to bring yourself to care at all. That's okay. It's Jesus's job to be perfect—not yours. Your job is simply to do the best you can every single day to make Him your number one priority in everything that you do. And then tomorrow, to do the same thing all over again.

While doing some research for this book, I asked the question on Facebook: "I'm curious--what things have you given up because you're a Christian? (Both the obvious and not so obvious.)" The answers varied, but none of them really surprised me. Trashy books, TV shows and movies, doing whatever feels good at the time, bad relationships, premarital sex, wearing revealing clothing, negative thought patterns, unhealthy coping mechanisms, friendships... these were all things people had to give up, and I'm sure not all of them were easy!

One thing that did surprise me as I was reading through everyone's comments, though, was their reaction to having given these things up. Most people didn't comment on how difficult these things had been to let go of or how much they missed them. No one complained or grumbled. Instead, they all seemed truly joyful and made comments such as "I don't feel like I've really given anything up because I've gained so much more" and "Everything I have had to give up pales in [comparison to] what I have received!"

No, making God your number one priority is never going to be easy. But it will get easier. And I can promise you: it is worth it. What do you have to lose?

Made in United States
Troutdale, OR
06/19/2024